GRATITUDE

Gaëtan Chapoteau

Cover Image Credit: Philippe Attie

Disclaimer

All contents of this book are for informational and educational purposes only. The author is not in any way accountable for any results or outcomes that emanate from using this material. Constructive attempts have been made to provide information that is both accurate and effective, but the author is not bound for the accuracy or use/misuse of this information.

Dedication

To my beloved parents, Antoine Chapoteau and Nancy Leconte-Chapoteau for the hard work, dedication, commitment, and self-sacrifices you made for me. Mom, I'm thankful for your friendship, your continued and endless support, encouragement, your infinite patience, and unconditional love. Dad, I have silently watched and learned how you managed life, and you have been my unfailing guide. Thank you for your unconditional love and support. You have taught me to live by principles, without which I wouldn't have earned my success and for that, I'm forever grateful. This one's for you.

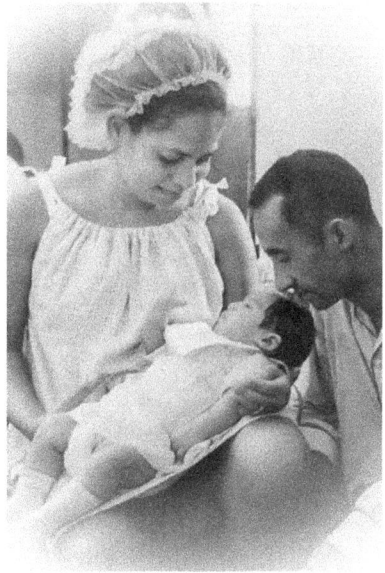

Introduction

Gratitude has been a long time coming. You see, I come from the Caribbean island of Haiti, from a small, desolate town called Gonaives. While my family was not the wealthiest, we were still considered the top one faction of the city's financial class. Our privilege became somewhat of a challenge for me; I spent years questioning the level of poverty around me while my family lived in abundance. I didn't take anything for granted, but I remember thinking that God was not fair to others. Why were only select groups of people wealthy? What made them different? Frequently, I felt unsettled; always wondering what my purpose was for being able to live how I was. Growing up, I ultimately knew that my family and I had to escape the confines of Gonaives. I realized that by relocating to Port-au-Prince, our country's capital, it would create a significant and positive change in our lives.

When I was 14, my dream came true. My brother Fabian and I moved to Port-au-Prince at first, followed by my brother Vladimir and sister Méroudji a few months later. I made many more friends there, and I had more family around me. The strange feeling still lingered, though. No matter what amount of greatness surrounded me, I always craved more.

I knew that I needed–and deserved–more out of life. Before relocating to Port-au-Prince, I had the opportunity to visit Miami, Fl. From that point on, I couldn't wait to make this magical city my home sooner. And so, after some time, I did.

I did what I had to do; I made the necessary endeavors to move to my dream city. While I faced many struggles along the way, finally, in 1992, I chose to alter my beliefs. Rather than having the mindset that everything must be perfect, I learned that trusting that things will always work out would be far better.

Before embarking on my voyage to the land of the free and home of the brave, I dedicated hours in local libraries researching books on self-development, psychology, and mysticism. I ended up discovering a gem that would forever change my life: The Science of Getting Rich by Wallace D. Wattles. It comprised the art of building wealth as a science, which I hadn't realized was exactly the concept I'd needed. I knew that my desire to live in Miami fueled from this hunger that dwelled deep within. What I didn't grasp at first was my devotion to becoming successful once the move was complete. As I continued my research and delved through the pages of my latest find, I considered that I could gain the abundant life I imagined, as long as I stayed on track.

I continuously studied *The Science of Getting Rich* with a burning hunger. I re-read it constantly and began practicing what I'd learned. I connected each of the principles strategically and began receiving results instantly. Things were already getting so much better, and this was only the beginning. It felt like a breath of fresh air. Eventually, I ended up reaching a point where I even considered praying as a distraction. Thus, I dropped all spiritual beliefs and focused wholeheartedly on driving the best results for my business.

Within three years of moving to Miami, I'd successfully built my first business from the ground up and was on my way to earn my first million dollars in revenue within the first year on conception. It was smooth sailing; I was a self-made man. From then on, I expanded my income considerably over the next few years. As I worked through expanding my company, time flew by. I began losing enthusiasm and grew tired of chasing the next big deal. So, following some extreme and strenuous moments of reflection, I decided that my life was better off without a business that required so much of me. It was taking a toll on my health, body, mind, and soul. Was I wrong about the way I went about life? The stunning revelation finally hit me: I had lost my sense of serenity that I'd worked so hard to achieve. I felt jailed; stuck to an idea that was doing me more harm than good. I was not willing to lose myself to my career, no matter how much success and money it promised. I decided that enough was enough. One day, without alerting anyone, I closed up shop. That was that.

It took me a couple of years to fully understand that shutting down my business was an impulsive, brazen move–complete with an abundance of guilt and disappointment. During the next 15 years that followed, I continued dwelling on the decisions that had led me to my current place in life. What actions had caused me to lose that priceless feeling of pure harmony, peace, and fulfillment, in which I began my journey? How did I get here? Most importantly: how could I get out of this rut?

One day, as my oldest son, Kristofer, and I discussed my past, he peppered me with questions in which I wasn't prepared for.

"What happened to you, Dad? How did you go from being so high-volume in life to now contemplating your very existence in the world?"

My son unintentionally hit me where it hurt. Worst of all, he was right. Kristofer exposed a truth in which

I didn't realize beneath I was hiding. As I considered my response, I grew dumbfounded. I ended up sharing my hidden secret after all those years with him.

I shared my journey on how I discovered my fate by analyzing *The Science of Getting Rich* during my youth. I went on to explain the loss that I was now feeling, my pride completely shot. It seemed as though I wasn't able to comprehend my loss of enthusiasm for anything. Instead, I felt a hole where my connection with my inner being should be. How could I have let this happen? This book was my holy grail, my sacred place to discover balance and replenish my motivation.

As if reading my mind, my eldest son then asked me, "Well, if you're so sure about that, why don't you just re-read the book to remind yourself what you've missed?"

This conversation occurred fifteen years after I'd first read the book that changed my life. After everything, it never occurred to me that perhaps reading it again, as a different man in a different part of his life, would make a difference. I knew right then and there that it was time to reread it, this time with a fresh pair of eyes and a newfound sense of optimism.

While finishing up the book a few weeks after our chat, I was appalled to realize that I'd completely omitted one of the most important concepts that I'd once learned: Gratitude, (covered in Chapter 7 of the book).

I battled with the idea and questioned the value of being thankful for some outside source that I couldn't distinguish from my persona. I noticed that I was missing that key ingredient to a successful life. All the money I had earned, all the achievements I'd received, everything I'd accomplished was all for nothing if I could not be thankful for them. My obsession with being the best was just that: an obsession. After all, I was the one responsible for my life choices and outcomes; wasn't it enough to be appreciative of myself?

After further contemplation, I realized I had much to re-learn and knew I had to find a way to share this gained knowledge and insight with others. Therefore, the burning desire to write this book bloomed within my soul like a flower ready to share its beauty with the world. I yearned to share the key component that was missing in my formula to success. As the great Roman philosopher, Marcus Tullius Cicero once said, "Gratitude is not only the greatest of virtues but the parent of all others."

Dear Reader,

I share with you my knowledge, my experiences, and my insight that we take for granted daily. May you never forget where you came from. May you always remember to stay on the right path. No matter what, always be humble. Remember: being greedy never let anyone stay at the top of their game for long. Know when you need to stop and restart yourself to get back to where you need to be.

Lastly, I want to share my thanks. Thank you for picking up this book and allowing it to enter your thoughts. I hope that it provides you with the words that you need to understand yourself. I hope it reminds you to always stay grateful throughout your life. Best of luck in all of your endeavors (and don't forget to thank your loved ones and the speed bumps along the way).

Thank you.

Gaëtan Chapoteau

Contents

ONE

Theory of Gratitude

"When a person doesn't have gratitude, something is missing in his or her humanity."
–Elie Wiesel

Background

Gratitude has so many various interpretations that people often lose the practicality of it all. It is a universal subject matter, mainly because it is not culturally or natively biased. Rather, it lies in the core of nature itself. Gratitude does more good than harm, and its virtue has enhanced many relationships, whether personal or professional. It has many forms according to who, what, or how it's expressed, and it embodies the feeling of being appreciative for all that is.

Application of Gratitude is efficiently focusing on the things that are going well in one's life. Furthermore, it involves making a commitment and observing the positive impact that lasts on everyone who practices. Expressing Gratitude is purposefully moving your focus from negative to positive and allowing that inner voice to reflect this genuine expression to others. While some may view life's challenges as a reason to feel resentment or bitterness, the real gift lies within those who consider each of these moments as a blessing in disguise. Developing this dimension of appreciation involves reflecting on past troubles with a fresh perspective, allowing one to view the future with a certainty of good things to come. Quite often, the thought of being grateful entails appreciating someone for the good they have done for us or the things we have received from them, yet it is so much more than that. To expand further, Gratitude embodies the feeling of genuinely appreciating who we are, where we are, and what we have. Unfortunately, for most people, they have to reach a certain point in their lives where everything seems to take a turn for the worse for them to realize just how good they once had it. Practicing Gratitude allows us the enlightenment of recognizing that we are enough. Whether substantial or immaterial, it is imperative to always be thankful for what we have.

Value of Gratitude

"In ordinary life, we hardly realize that we receive a great deal more than we give and that it is only with gratitude that life becomes rich." –Dietrich Bonhoeffer.

What a strong sentiment that certainly rings true; we regularly underestimate the very things that most merit our appreciation. It took me a while before I could fully grasp this concept. The Spirit of Gratitude was dormant in my life until I encountered peculiar situations which triggered and illuminated my inner light. At last, I could formulate feasible solutions to the problematic situations I faced.

To fully express appreciation, awareness is vital. It involves being mindful of gifts that we ordinarily underestimate and keying into the multitude of purposes behind each act of kindness. The abundant road of gratitude lies on each of our paths; it's up to us to create the direction that leads us there.

When it comes down to Gratitude, individuals tend to feel this emotion according to their current mood or state. The person's frame of mind frequently reflects on how deep their expression of Gratitude lies. All modes of recognition lead to self-improvement in one way or another. For instance, imagine a student receiving a gift from their teacher and then immediately accepting it and walking away. While the teacher may feel unacknowledged due to lack of appreciation, this seemingly small gesture may defer her from giving her students gifts in the future for fear of being taken advantage of and simultaneously not feeling appreciated. However, looking at the situation in a different light, let's pretend the student did appreciate the gift. Two things would happen immediately: first, the teacher would feel motivated and glad to give to such a deserving, grateful student. Second, the probability of the boy or another student receiving more gifts in the future has suddenly increased. People tend to feel far more thankful when they realize someone has reasonable expectations when giving rather than if the other person expects something in return.

Individuals can utilize the gift of gratitude to shape new social relations or to expand upon and improve current ones. Demonstrations of such can be used to ask for forgiveness, make amends, or help address different issues individuals may face. Naturally, the beauty of being thankful for merely being alive is an excellent method to inspire oneself to secure the day full of positivity. Tomorrow isn't guaranteed; therefore, we must make the most of each day.

Another perspective of Gratitude alludes to recognizing an advantage or opportunity when presented, regardless of who or where it derived. Take the time to be appreciative for the endeavors, sacrifices, and deeds that someone else in your life endured for your advantage. Whenever you're feeling down, it is imperative to realize that you have what it takes to lift yourself back up again. There is always something to be grateful for; it's up to you to delve deep and home in on all in which you possess.

Setting aside time each day to reflect on life's simple blessings sets into motion certain self-restoring forms that produce exceptional results. It is essential to realize that Gratitude does not necessarily rely on hypothetical life situations. It sometimes involves an informed decision. For example, we can still be appreciative, notwithstanding when our feelings and emotions aren't in the best place, such as being hurt or angry. Rather than focusing on the negative, we must make the conscious effort to alter our state of mind by instead focusing on the right things.

Most often, Gratitude is spiritually inclined; it is a divine being. As the American religious leader and lawyer James E. Faust once declared, "As with all commandments, gratitude is a description of a successful mode of living." A thankful heart opens our eyes to a multitude of blessings that continually surround us.

TWO

Aptitude for Gratitude

*"The future depends on attitude, aptitude, and gratitude--
not on knowledge."*
–Debasish Mridha M.D.

Aptitude is the natural capacity to accomplish something. Many of us are familiar with the fact that it is critical to have a knack for gratitude. While it is natural to be appreciative for something that comes to fruition, it is difficult to be thankful for the speed bumps that occur along the way. What many folks fail to realize is that these challenges are all a part of our ultimate journey to happiness, and it is vital to appreciate these bumps in the road just as much as the final result. It's all about the pursuit of happiness.

One's sense of obligation is conceived from intimacy and is steadfast. In other words, the feeling of commitment to someone or something depends on the relationship between them, and it is authentic. That genuine connection shared with a loved one reinforces the act of both parties feeling grateful for one another.

Speaking from experience, it is challenging to be in a gloomy state and be appreciative at the same time. However, it is possible; it's merely a matter of always being mindful of having that "feel good" state of mind. Many agree that it is hard to continually stay thankful, discovering that their wave of attitude towards gratitude is like the tides of the sea, indicated by what's currently going on in their life. For those with negative emotions from an early age, a large portion of their existence is conditioned with fear.

Aptitude is a natural propensity in our mindset that indicates the likelihood of our accomplishments later in life. Consequently, many of us share a profound desire to value everything in a positive light. Aptitude is not limited to our state of mind alone; it's the way we've been programmed throughout our lives and how it reflects in our everyday choices. Aptitude is an inclination combined with action that demonstrates one's manner.

Gratitude is a highly dominant activity and is one of the most regarded uses of empowerment. As referenced earlier, it is challenging to be in a negative state and still feel thankful, yet it is much more difficult if deep down inside lies a lingering feeling of doom or gloom. Gratitude must be embedded within our soul, almost like a piece of the puzzle that completes us a whole. Once the conscious decision is made to accept and embrace Gratitude fully, fear or doubt will forever be banished, and your life will change drastically for the better. With enough practice, an Aptitude for Gratitude can be acquired. Once an individual realizes the plenitude they currently have, positive changes will immediately ensue.

Let's imagine for a moment that we only have a day left to live. How incredible does it feel now, to simply exist? Imagine how drastically the world would change if everyone had this exact state of mind: happy to live. It is essential to remind ourselves of all the complimentary items in which we are gifted: the simple act of breathing, our health, our surroundings, and of course, our friends and family. The mere ability to dwell within the human body is a tremendous blessing within itself. When we take a moment to appreciate the small things in life, our perspective becomes far more extensive and broadened.

For those who choose to live in a constant state of anger, disappointment, or bitterness, they fail to realize that they are consciously living in misery when they can be living a life full of joy, love, and contentment. Predisposition is a difficult barrier to breach; however, the best way to tackle this obstacle is by achieving an authentic Aptitude for Gratitude. Think about it: astonishing delight is all around us! Take the time to grasp this concept in all of its glorified simplicity.

How frequently do we express our appreciation for anything or anyone these days? Whether verbally or nonverbally, the notion somehow transforms into a psychological concept, losing all sense of direction and purpose. Generally, many people feel that something extraordinary must occur to feel excited enough to express it out loud. Offering thanks is a fundamental component to make our reality a more joyful place and should be practiced often, no matter how small the feat. Not only will we feel great for doing so, but it can also brighten someone else's day.

Many people appreciate the beauty of giving more than receiving. Take Christmas Day, for example, the pure joy in a parent's heart as they watch their child open the gift that they've been asking Santa for all year. Accepting a declaration of Gratitude is the equivalent of receiving a blessing. If you're still struggling to obtain an Aptitude for Gratitude, you must train your mind to be grateful for every little thing received.

Below are some techniques to help master achieving an ability for appreciation.

MAKE A COMMITMENT TO EXERCISE GRATITUDE: Research proves that committing to something enhances the probability of completing the task–yet another fact that can be used to our advantage. Begin a personal appreciation pledge, something as simple as starting each day by declaring, "I promise to remember my good fortune today." Post it somewhere convenient where it will be easy to note each day.

PRACTICE GRATITUDE-RELATED PRAYERS: In many religions, prayers of appreciation are regarded as the most dominant type of worship. Throughout these prayers, one can perceive clarity as to who they are, what they have, and all there is in which to appreciate.

MAINTAIN A GRATITUDE DIARY: Begin a daily practice to remember the blessings, opportunities, and experiences allotted to you. Each night, ideally before going to bed so that the positivity lingers throughout your slumber, reserve a few precious moments to jot down at least three things to be grateful for from that day.

REMEMBER THE BAD TIMES, TOO: Being appreciative of your current situation helps when recalling the bad times previously endured along the way. When remembering them, it is a beautiful feeling to reflect on just how much progress has transpired since then. Being mindful of remembering the bad times helps you become more appreciative of where you currently are in life. Value mistakes for their ability to teach you. After all, they're merely learning experiences that benefit us later on in life.

UTILIZE VISUAL REMINDERS: As the two main obstacles of thankfulness are neglect and an absence of careful mindfulness, visual aids can be used as signals to activate notions of gratitude. These visual aids can be anything from another individual to a Gratitude journal.

MAKE AN EFFORT: Whenever a smile appears on your face, it is essential to recognize what you can appreciate at that precise moment. To go above and beyond, practice gestures of appreciation such as smiling, saying thanks, or composing letters of appreciation. These seemingly small gestures will ultimately make a world of difference in your life.

CONSIDER SOME FRESH POSSIBILITIES:
When you have the opportunity to make the most out
of a thoughtful gesture, seize the moment to
acknowledge the positive vibes around you. Trust me;
it will do your heart well.

EXPRESS GRATITUDE TOWARD YOURSELF:
Gratitude isn't solely based on someone else's actions
towards you. On the contrary, it revolves around you.
Give yourself a well-deserved pat on the back for the
wondrous occasions in which you treat yourself. For
instance, did you allow yourself to a great night's
sleep? If so, go you!

IT CHANGES YOUR POINT OF VIEW: Should
you find yourself in a position where you feel that
nothing is going right, place yourself in the shoes of
somebody who is encountering setbacks more
noteworthy than your own. Remember that the
universe would never throw you in a position that you
are unable to handle. Stay humble throughout your life
journey.

THREE

Diary of Gratitude

"I always say, keep a diary, and someday it'll keep you."
–Mae West

Imagine a scenario where there's one straightforward approach to make you more joyful throughout the day. Sounds unrealistic, right? It turns out that there is, in fact, one easy practice that will always make your glass half full: maintaining a diary of Gratitude. A diary of Gratitude is a personal journal consisting of written sentiments in which one is thankful. People who concentrate on the significant things in their world utilize these logs daily to their advantage. Research shows that individuals who are consistently appreciative are overall much happier than those who are less humble. Furthermore, sentiments of appreciation may even have mental and physical benefits. A diary is a great way to relieve tension by releasing stress through the powerful use of words.

Writing helps us focus on the brighter things in life that we may otherwise overlook. Many times, we become oblivious to the good stuff that life throws at us, simply because our minds are consumed by the bad. It's understandable; things happen and get in the way. It's a part of life. However, by shifting your mindset and allowing yourself to write a couple of minutes each day, you'll be pleasantly surprised with the positive outcome that will follow. By keeping a record of all the positive light in your life, you'll begin noticing change all around you. You'll feel more enthusiastic, joyful, and full of life.

Everyone's gratitude journal will vary in content. Some may focus on the positive that happened during the day, while others might choose to describe their entire weekend. The most important concept is to select an outline that works best for you and your way of life. If you have limited time and can't dedicate to writing full paragraphs, consider bullet points instead. These short, sweet, and to the point topics help you view your ideas in a brighter light and are a great writing strategy for those who are always on the go.

Whether you use your phone or the good ol' pen and paper routine, remember to stay consistent. By doing so, you'll stay on track and log everything in which you're appreciative. The trick is to carry it out with determination and purpose. Remember: it's just you and your thoughts; there are no right or wrong answers.

Always write to your heart's content and keep things straightforward, like mentioning a meal you just had with an old friend or investing in a gym membership. Reflect on what is going well in your life, and you'll soon notice that extra pep in your step. Spending a minimum of five minutes each day has proven effective. You'll feel happier as you take the time to practice self-care, and soon enough, you'll be living your dream lifestyle. Contrary to having an average diary consisting of your day's adventures and your thoughts, a gratitude journal can transform your life and the lives of those around you. Below are some useful tips that will make your Gratitude diary a hit.

UTILIZE YOUR DIARY OF GRATITUDE TO START A CONVERSATION: It's easy to be engaged in conversations that include gossip, antagonism, and cynicism; it's almost like our mind's way of attempting to make ourselves feel better about our lives. Sadly, these types of discussions are generally inefficient and a waste of time. Changing the topic to a more positive note, like mentioning some good news you recently received, can inspire yourself and the people with whom you are conversing. Going forward, each time you're involved in a conversation, make a conscious effort to infuse positivity into the discussion. Bring up how pleasant the climate is, the tasty food you just finished eating, or how much you relish hanging out with your friends during leisure time.

SHARE YOUR GRATITUDE WITH LOVED ONES: You may be indebted for something your friends, colleagues, or significant other does for you, yet appreciation will feel significantly more dominant when you are grateful for their character. For instance, acknowledge that your roommate took out the garbage, or when a friend picks up the tab at dinner. You'll be more appreciative of what they do because it shows how much they care. Always take note of the little things that your loved ones do for you and keep your diary handy. Next time you see them, pause for a minute to share how they make you feel and how happy you are that they are in your life.

UTILIZE YOUR DIARY OF GRATITUDE TO WRITE THANK-YOU CARDS: Take the time to write a note expressing thanks to others. For an added touch, consider making your card instead of heading to your local Hallmark store and buying one. That extra touch of love will be seen and highly regarded. Remember to check back in with your Gratitude diary to uncover something you previously jotted down and might have forgotten about them. Work it into the note as you give thanks, then snail mail it to them. They'll view it as a pleasant surprise that you went the extra mile to show your love and support.

ALLOW GRATITUDE TO CHANGE A NEGATIVE OUTLOOK INTO A POSITIVE ONE: Think about a period in your life that was an intense or depressing experience. Pause for a minute to run through your diary to check whether you can discover something you are thankful for because of this experience. Did it help you in any capacity? Were you able to grow and learn as a result? Perhaps it even helped you gain the perspective to comfort another person who is facing a similar encounter. Taking the positive out of any negative situation and helping others will allow your inner smile to shine, knowing that you're doing the right thing.

To make a compelling diary of Gratitude, make a list of what you are thankful for and review it daily. Here's a simple example:

WHAT I'M GRATEFUL FOR:

- My Family
- My Friends (Be specific! Enter names here.)
- My Teacher
- My Business (or Job)
- My Senses
- My Health
- Awesome Memories
- My Pets

The list goes on and on, and the longer it is, the happier you'll feel when rereading them. While sometimes it may be challenging to get through a tough time, looking back through your diary will exhibit just how much you've been blessed. Our minds react more to quality over quantity. When someone has an Aptitude for Gratitude, the diary content can and will be a long list. Dig deep into your diary, even the smaller things, to enable you to fortify Gratitude in your life. You'll notice as your brain and body become acclimated to experiencing appreciation. The more profound you feel for even the smallest things in life, the more natural your Aptitude for Gratitude enhances. Keep that momentum going throughout your day, every day!

One of the best times to write is right before you go to sleep because it will end your day on a high note. It signals your intuition and encourages you to insert a positive outlook into your soul. In the morning, take a quick moment to glance at your journal. See that smile? It's happiness in the making. It's the feeling that everything is going to be okay, and that today will be another great day.

FOUR

Ineffectiveness of Hollow

Gratitude

"Silent gratitude isn't very much use to anyone."
–Gertrude Stein

We have lost so much due to our lack of appreciation. We've forgotten that a simple "thank you" rather than a weak, measly, "much appreciated" can leave anyone feeling great. By expanding your mind and developing a positive outlook for everything that comes your way will enable you to experience exceptional levels of content. Many situations in life require you to summon positive feelings of Gratitude and appreciation. What we don't realize is that this admiration ends up becoming an essential role in all that we do.

From personal experience, I've found that countless people are only truly grateful when they get what they want. It's like a one-way ticket to instant gratification. However, it's just that: instant gratification: that small moment in the day where we got our way. Here's to hoping that it impacts more than just that moment. As humans, we understand that life has its ups and downs. Therefore, we must show a deep level of gratefulness towards all encounters in life because they did, of course, make us the person we are today. I had my very own encounter with this lesson during a recent trip to Barcelona.

The Case of The Lost Camera

In the summer of 2018, my family and I traveled to Europe. One day, while in Barcelona, Spain, with my two oldest boys Kristofer, Xavier, and their friend, Alec, we took the train one afternoon to meet with the remainder of our family. Of course, we somehow ended up on the wrong wagon. Rather than seat 14B of wagon six, we were on number eight. During the time spent going back and forth, trying to find our proper seats, I managed to leave my camera behind on the wrong wagon.

When we arrived in Madrid, we rented a car, had dinner, and headed to Avila, just two hours away. The next morning, when I realized I hadn't seen my camera since our return, I was shocked to learn I must've misplaced it. *Damn it!* I knew I could just replace it, but it wasn't about the camera. The pictures and memories it contained were far more valuable than the small hunk of metal itself. All those countless adventures captured by photos were now gone, inevitably lost forever.

I shared my dilemma with the woman of my life, Alejandra, who responded with, "Didn't I give you that camera for your birthday? How could you be so careless and lose it already?" I calmly explained that I could always buy a new one. I could sense her disappointment as she said, "Is that so? That means you were never grateful for it–as if the camera wasn't good enough for you. That's how you sound right now!"

I understood her feelings but knew the camera itself wasn't the case. My point was valid; of course, I could buy another camera, but money can't buy memories. My boys and I created a bond that would always tie us together, captured by the selfies we snapped as we shared endless laughs. How could those moments ever be recreated?

Two days passed by. I was strolling the avenues of Madrid with my boys, lamenting the camera when a notification pinged on my phone. Someone had sent me a direct message on Instagram: "Did you lose a camera?" *Was this happening?* There was still good in this world, after all! I had goosebumps all over. Shocked, I responded, "What? Who is this?" She replied, "I'm sorry, but I had a look at your pictures, which is how I found you. If it's you who lost your camera, I have it, and know that it's in good hands."

That same individual also messaged my son, Xavier, stating that she found our camera and requested that we contact her. I couldn't believe it. I stared at my boys, who knew my thoughts on Gratitude, as we had ironically discussed it an hour earlier. I had told Kristofer that I wanted to return to that place where I once was when things were so perfect and smooth. Right then and there, I understood what was missing: thoughtfulness.

After an hour, the woman who found the camera called. Kristofer exclaimed, "That was quick, Dad! We were just talking about it!" The fact that someone reached out to us to have discovered the camera was amazing. My curiosity was piqued; how had this person found the camera and found us? I reassured myself that I would receive answers soon enough.

In the meantime, I responded to this person who was now my saving grace, asking when and where she could meet. This happened on a Tuesday; we would be flying back to Miami on Thursday. We kept exchanging messages with the woman who kept my memories. She was at work, so her responses were understandably delayed. Finally, we'd agreed to meet at 9 PM that night at the well-known church, *La Sagrada Família*, in Barcelona.

I considered the expense of having the camera packed and shipped to Florida, which would take a couple of days and cost around 200 euros. So, I concluded that it would be best to go to Barcelona. I had about twenty-four hours to go, come back, and return just in time for our flight on Thursday morning. Naturally, I was weary about the whole scenario, especially after speaking with my close friend Clifton. "Be careful, brother; this might be too good to be true. Make sure you don't go into an alley, stay around people, and meet in a public place." Hopefully, my friend was wrong, and it would be a simple exchange with a kind-hearted soul.

My mind was reeling as I waited for the train to Barcelona on Wednesday morning. I kept wondering how on earth they'd found the camera. *Could this be a trap?* At about 10:30 AM, I took the train and headed for Barcelona. I got there at about 12:45 PM, took a taxi and at 1 PM, I messaged the person that I was at our appointed meeting ground. She showed up within five minutes, a little bag dangling in her hand. Since she had already seen my pictures, she recognized me immediately. She walked towards me, smiling. She drew closer, exclaiming, "Your camera!" as she gave me the bag. We ended up embracing in a tight hug. I instantly grew teary-eyed; how could I ever thank her?

She introduced herself to me as Gabriela. I can't tell you how many times I said, "thank you," all the while smiling from ear to ear. At last, I asked her, "How did you find my camera?" She began recounting her discovery, explaining that her cousin Angelina had initially found the camera while she traveled from Madrid to Barcelona. Angelina was returning home from a trip and told Gabriela that she'd found a camera on the train. They decided that they had to find the original owner, knowing how much the owner must miss his camera. "That's when I began looking at the pictures; I had to uncover the mystery of its owner!"

She revealed to me that the first thing she did was call Sony to check if the serial number registered to anyone. Oddly, it was not. She continued and described how she delved through the photos and saw a vehicle with a Mexican license plate number. Gabriela called the Mexico Transportation Department to run the license plate number and discover who the tag belonged to. Unfortunately, this too led to a dead end, but Gabriela was determined. She continued scrolling through the pictures for useful information and came across an image of Kristofer wearing a T-shirt with a hashtag ENTRPRNR on it in front of the Eiffel Tower. Gabriela then searched the hashtag ENTRPRNR on Instagram and found the image with us from a couple of hash-tagged posts. My sons and I had all posted the photo, so she was able to locate our accounts. From there, she sent the three of us direct messages, knowing it must be us who lost the camera.

To this day, I'm still in shock. The amount of sleuthing and hope on this stranger's behalf to find the actual camera owner is astonishing. Thank goodness that the woman who made the discovery was an honest, genuine soul.

Stunned and dumbfounded, I kept staring at Gabriela with a ginormous smile on my face when she said, "Be thankful; that's all you have to do. Don't lose sight of all the wonderful people out there. I don't want your money, either."

Ironically, as she said this, I was simultaneously calculating how much money I should give her. Perhaps the original price of the camera? I was still doing the math in my head when she stopped me. "I don't expect anything in return. Just be grateful that the camera made its way back to you."

This world is tremendous. It's full of millions of people; many who tend to forget to be thoughtful and kind. I easily could've been taken advantage of, but instead, the encounter ended up becoming a life lesson. Because of this, I learned to appreciate my mistakes instead of getting angry at myself.

That exchange was a divine moment in my life. I shared my thoughts with Gabriela, letting her know that I chose to give up on the situation versus practicing gratitude. She smiled at me. "If you ever find yourself doubting whether you should do good in this world, think back to this moment." Then she asked, "What are you doing next?" I told her I was going to wait for the train back to Madrid. "Since you have some time, let's celebrate your reunion with your camera!" I gladly agreed and asked what she had in mind. She proceeded to tell me about the Festival of Cataluña and a Barca soccer match at the Camp Nou Stadium. "Messi playing on the field would be quite an experience!" I beamed. We merrily watched the soccer match, our hearts full of gratitude.

I'll always remember that fateful encounter with a smile and will forever practice what Gabriela taught me that day. Meister Eckhart once said, "If the only prayer you said in your whole life was 'thank you,' that would suffice."

The majority of us think of appreciation as a mere "thank you" to someone who has assisted us or offered us a gift. Gratitude isn't just an activity; it's a positive, exceptional feeling that fills a need. Showing shallow appreciation can result in the following outcomes:

BEING GRATEFUL VERSUS PESSIMISTIC THOUGHTS: Frequently, people that are depressed don't see the positive in their world. They have these invisible blinders blocking their mind from viewing the light at the end of the tunnel. Perhaps they believe that being sad is easier than being happy. They forget to remember all of the awesome things that happen to them daily, choosing instead to reflect on the person that cut them off in traffic, or the barista giving them the wrong order. It's okay; this happens to everyone. It still happens to me every once in a while. I throw myself a pity party and think the world is out to get me. Allowing pessimistic thoughts to drift through your mind doesn't benefit anyone. When you feel yourself heading in this direction, take a moment to think of three good things that happened to you that day. You'll be smiling in no time!

BEING GRATEFUL VERSUS LOW CONFIDENCE: An ungrateful heart undoubtedly triggers low confidence. These individuals are not appreciative of the person they were made to be. It's easy to stay fixated in that troubled mindset. How often have we looked in the mirror and scorned ourselves for what we saw? How can we make this better? It's simple: practice self-care and learn to love the person you are. The universe gives you minor inconveniences not to ruin your life, but to teach you a lesson. Be thankful for your journey.

BEING GRATEFUL VERSUS COVETNESS: In the end, the feeling of greed can endanger everything you have and want from life. It's not a healthy way to live. There is no need to fill the void of lust and greed. Seldom do the people who act this way get what they want. Stay on the right path in life and consider that the end goal will be well worth the wait.

BEING GRATEFUL VERSUS BITTER ATTITUDE: Those who have a negative mentality tend to struggle with forgiving. Their thoughts become foggy, making it difficult to forgive others and even themselves. Forgiveness is one of those major concepts in which people struggle. When someone holds onto a grudge, they fail to realize just how toxic they're being by keeping all of those feelings within. Acknowledge when you or someone you know is dealing with a situation that requires forgiving. Take a step back to evaluate the situation before making any harsh judgments.

BE GRATEFUL FOR YOUR FUTURE: So many opportunities pass by because people couldn't be grateful when they needed to be. Don't let this happen to you. Instead, take a moment to contemplate everything that you did to get to where you are. Your future holds countless possibilities; use this to your advantage.

FIVE

Gratitude to Supreme Being

"If the only prayer you said in your whole life was "thank you,"
that would suffice."
–Meister Eckhart

Gratitude is an essential element of various religions, and research has explored potential connections between personal religious beliefs and gratitude with multiple outcomes. Appreciation lies in the core of many spiritual traditions where giving thanks is considered second nature.

Because of this behavior, individuals become associated with each other in a spiritual light. The ultimate objective is to reflect on the good things that one has received by intently looking for opportunities to give back. The spiritual aspect of appreciation defies a selfish conviction that one merits or is qualified for the gifts, blessings, and opportunities that one receives. Understanding the lives that others live is a significant acknowledgment and reminds us to be humble.

Genuine appreciation drives individuals to encounter life circumstances transparently, inspiring them to get involved with the community to share and build together.

Long before psychology, researchers realized that gratitude is an important matter to study, yet another group of scholars beat them to it. These individuals preached the significance of recognition, demonstrating that Gratitude has a special place in this world and all the lives that inhabit it.

According to research, most people have an inherent engagement in religious activities. By having a personal relationship with God or their higher power, it exhibits religious commitment and helps one achieve spiritual transcendence. Many religions believe in the practice of speaking a prayer of gratitude each morning. Positive affirmations also help guide you into having a spectacular day. All you need are words of wisdom to help guide you.

I like to start each morning standing tall, facing the sun. Next, I repeat this phrase out loud, "Mighty God in me; I now face your eternal sunrise and receive your mighty radiance and activity. Visibly manifest in my experience now." It truly helps me to be the best person I can be. Find a phrase that resonates with your soul and let it give you light.

With children, it's quite common to see parents teach them gratitude from a young age. It's essential for parents to talk to their children about helping those less fortunate than themselves.

Alan Cohen once said, "Gratitude, like faith, is a muscle. The more you use it, the stronger it grows, and the more power you have to use it on your behalf. If you do not practice gratefulness, its assistance will go unnoticed, and your capacity to draw on its gifts will be diminished."

I once decided to cut off praying to start focusing more on my business. As a result, I ended up becoming disconnected from my inner being. Initially, I thought that I had made the right decision. In fact, for several months, things ran smoothly. I wasn't aware that I had paralyzed my inner harmony and cut off my source of happiness until I began to lose my peace of mind. Nothing in this world can give you lasting joy and happiness if you are not working from your heart and soul. I started to lose profit in my business, making it harder to stay on the right path.

I learned that it is essential to give thanks to God, as the Bible so emphasizes. Psalms 100:4 says, "Enter into His gates with thanksgiving, and into His courts with praise: be thankful unto Him and bless His name." Showing your appreciation towards your higher power by giving, singing, praising, and, acknowledging Him as the ultimate provider are some examples. Once I returned my focus to what was truly important, my life made more sense. The sense of security and peace of mind that followed this decision was life-altering.

SIX

Beneficial Effects of Gratitude

"Gratitude opens the door to the power, the wisdom, and the creativity of the universe. You open the door through gratitude."
–Deepak Chopra

Practicing Gratitude has tremendous benefits; the depth in which you practice determines the results you enjoy. In other words, you reap what you sow. The following are a few examples of good outcomes by practicing appreciation:

IT FORTIFIES RELATIONSHIPS: The more we realize the value of those around us, the more we are inclined to treat them better. Expressing Gratitude to someone will give you a more profound feeling of love. It strengthens bonds between neighbors, co-workers, classmates, etc. There is no chance of bitterness after being grateful for something or someone; instead, you'll feel even more joy and happiness. As you continue demonstrating your appreciation to those around you, you will frequently see that the dynamic of your relationships will take a robust and positive turn. Your bond will become more grounded, and the other individual will be increasingly open with their own emotions towards you, paving the way for a beautiful friendship.

IT ENCOURAGES OPTIMISM: When we are grateful for something we have; it becomes easier to have stronger faith that things will only get better. If everyone were to practice this belief, the world would be a much greater place. The idea is to make you feel great about everything that's yet to come, encouraging your emotions to stay focused and in a positive light.

IT IS BENEFICIAL FOR HEALTH: There is concrete proof that the act of saying 'thanks' is beneficial for your wellbeing. It's also an excellent method to avoid depression, on the basis that it supports an idealistic standpoint and gives the chance to concentrate on constructive life situations. Practicing Gratitude is also known to help battle anxiety and improve sleeping patterns, resulting in utmost tranquility. A good night's rest has an essential impact on your general wellbeing and is a crucial component of your daily schedule.

IT HELPS YOUR CAREER: Remember to enjoy the little things in life. By expressing Gratitude to everything and everyone around you, you're boosting your ambition, making your current state more pleasant. This extra boost will create a smooth path to achieve your career goals while simultaneously increasing both your leadership skills and profitability. Next thing you know, you're offered a promotion, pushing you to expand your horizons even further.

IT FORTIFIES YOUR POSITIVE FEELINGS: Gratitude supports mental stability by reinforcing your pleasant feelings. It diminishes the sentiments of envy, helps you build a constructive identity, promotes optimism, and makes you less materialistic. Your spirituality and confidence will soar, resulting in kind acts of love towards others.

IT EXPELS YOUR FEELING OF OWNERSHIP: This is easily a standout amongst the essential advantages of Gratitude. When you're thankful, you won't have a feeling that the world owes you anything.

It decreases your self-claim and enables you to work diligently.

IT IMPROVES YOUR UNDERSTANDING AND PATIENCE: Gratitude improves your psychological quality by expanding your compassion. When you show Gratitude, you'll feel relief by trusting that your dreams will work out as expected. You'll learn that you can't attain success in a day, so buckle up and enjoy the ride.

IT ENABLES YOU TO RELINQUISH THINGS THAT YOU CAN'T CONTROL: Gratitude encourages you to create mental strength that enables you to relinquish things that are out of your control. Thankful and rational thinking individuals can channel their vitality on things that they can change and ultimately let go of things that they cannot.

IT ENCOURAGES YOU TO LEARN FROM YOUR FLAWS: Appreciation encourages you to move on from your past mistakes and enables you to learn from them. When you're appreciative, you'll understand that you are fortunate to be given another opportunity in spite of your errors. Learning from mistakes makes us human. For instance, perhaps you failed an exam because you were out late the night before. Luckily, your professor is allowing you to retake the exam. How would you feel in this situation? An inner spark will ignite, urging you to study hard before your next test as opposed to heading off to the club for a wild night out.

IT TEACHES YOU TO ACCEPT CHANGE: Thankful and rationally strong-headed individuals realize that there's nothing perpetual in this world. They consider change to be an opportunity, so instead of opposing it, they accept it. They believe that change will open a mind-blowing new part of their life.

IT ENCOURAGES YOU TO PRACTICE SELF-ESTEEM AND SELF-SYMPATHY: Thankful individuals never beat themselves up; instead, they practice self-sympathy. They rest when necessary and man-up against any personal guilt.

IT MOTIVATES YOU TO UTILIZE YOUR TIME ACCORDINGLY: When you practice Gratitude, you understand that your time in this world is precious, so you utilize it carefully. Don't waste your time looking for somebody's endorsement or controlling another person's perception of you. As you absentmindedly scroll through social media or live vicariously through others by watching sleazy reality shows, you're only glorifying a false sense of identity. Gratitude enables you to concentrate on what's imperative. It engages you to utilize your time wisely, go after your dreams, and build meaningful relationships.

The list goes on and on. You'll soon discover the wonders of these benefits, and eventually, you'll help others by sharing these experiences with the world.

SEVEN

Gratitude and Wealth

"The grateful mind is constantly fixed upon the best. Therefore, it tends to become the best; it takes the form or character of the best and will receive the best."
~ **Wallace Wattles, Author** *(The Science of Getting Rich)*

Everyone needs to be held accountable for their thoughts and actions. Wealth comes when you succumb to a positive mindset. So, how can you acquire all the wealth? First, you must understand some of the main principles. See, the millionaire's frame of mind dependably follows an appreciative viewpoint. This perspective starts before they achieve success. To earn this wealth, you have to behave as if the universe or divine nature–depending on the way you see it–exists to give you what you truly desire. You have to believe you are deserving of what you get. Do not get fed up when things don't go your way. Instead, ask yourself, "How can I make this situation better?"

First and foremost: change your mindset. You associate what you have and equalize with it. People who are without this kind of progressive way of thinking end up destitute, living in shortage, not having the life they desire.

The most critical factor we overlook when striving for wealth is the role of Gratitude in its establishment and preservation. Wallace Wattles proffered a way out over a hundred years ago on how to get rich with the concept of Gratitude. *The Science of Getting Rich* shines the spotlight on the influence of our minds. We're all meant to flourish; the universe wants us to thrive! You need to accept this fact and whatever your circumstances, believe that you are improving each day. Acknowledge that the initial move towards an abundant lifestyle is to express your desires to your higher power.

I practiced the principles outlined in this book for years but ignored the crucial part in Chapter seven, where Wallace described the role of Gratitude in acquiring wealth.

For one to be entirely devoted to God, he must give thanks for every one of His gifts. We must be mindful not to enable the spirit of ingratitude to avoid dissociation with God and our loved ones. Nothing transforms us into harsh, narrow-minded, disgruntled individuals more rapidly than an unthankful soul. We appear to be never truly content with what we have, sufficient or insufficient, in good condition or vice-versa. We ought to consider this as a trial of our character.

Maintain a gracious frame of mind, even when you're not getting what you want. Whatever life throws at you is not in vain; it's all for a reason. Try not to consider your setbacks as a roadblock, but part of your adventure. As you continue expanding your expressions of Gratitude, negative feelings will begin to fade away from the spotlight.

Just remember that all you have doesn't make a difference if you don't value it! You'll never feel satisfied without Gratitude, regardless of the amount of money you have. So, paying little heed to your bank account and cultivating a habit of Gratitude is vital. As there are laws for almost every principle in this world, there is also a Law of Gratitude. When you practice authenticity, your devotion to God will only increase, bringing all that you want to fruition. We are all connected by a spiritual entity, and ultimately, it is our thoughts that form us and shape our outcomes. Don't spend your time ruminating on the mistakes you've made in the past. Direct your concentration to connect with your Creator and utilize the power and benefits that follow.

To create wealth from Gratitude and attitude, you have to be optimistic. Being bitter never helps anyone, whether to acquire wealth or otherwise. Denis Waitley made it quite clear when he said, "Happiness cannot be traveled to, owned, earned, worn or consumed. Happiness is the spiritual experience of living every minute, with love, grace, and gratitude." Gratitude isn't merchandise delivered in light of payment or a transaction carried out between two people. It is a reaction to a blessing.

In all things, there is heart, patience, love, and Gratitude. How will you use this information to transform your life?

"What are you grateful for today?"
–Anonymous

www.ingramcontent.com/pod-product-compliance
Lightning Source LLC
Chambersburg PA
CBHW051848090426
42811CB00034B/2254/J